The Weeping Degree

"THE WEEPING DEGREE IS A thoughtful set of poetry. ...a thoroughly engaging read. Sad in parts—I had a little cry here and there."

—Judge (female, 69) TWSA

"THIS BOOK HAS A GENTLE BUT powerful message. Some poems felt very relatable to me as I had a difficult start in life too. I loved the honesty and the accessibility. It's a difficult subject in many ways, but the author/poet did a good job of putting over her thoughts/feelings in a relatable and safe way."

—Judge (female, 60) TWSA

"A VERY ORIGINAL WAY of telling a very personal story."

—Judge (female, 55) TWSA

"A TOUCHING SET OF POETRY; so much so, I found myself rereading several of them."

—Judge (male, 44) TWSA

The Weeping Degree

HOW ASTROLOGY SAVED ME FROM SUICIDE

POEMS & PROSE

Kelly Watt

Wild Rising Press

EVERGREEN, COLORADO

The author gratefully acknowledges the financial assistance of the Ontario Arts
Council through an OAC recommender grant for this project.

Section Openers by Mary M. Meade based on astronomical diagrams from
1300–1500 part of medieval manuscripts held in the British Library in London.
Astrological wheel istock/Margo Kukhar.

Editor: Judyth Hill
Book Design: Mary M. Meade

www.wildrisingpress.com
ISBN 978-1-957468-32-7—First Edition

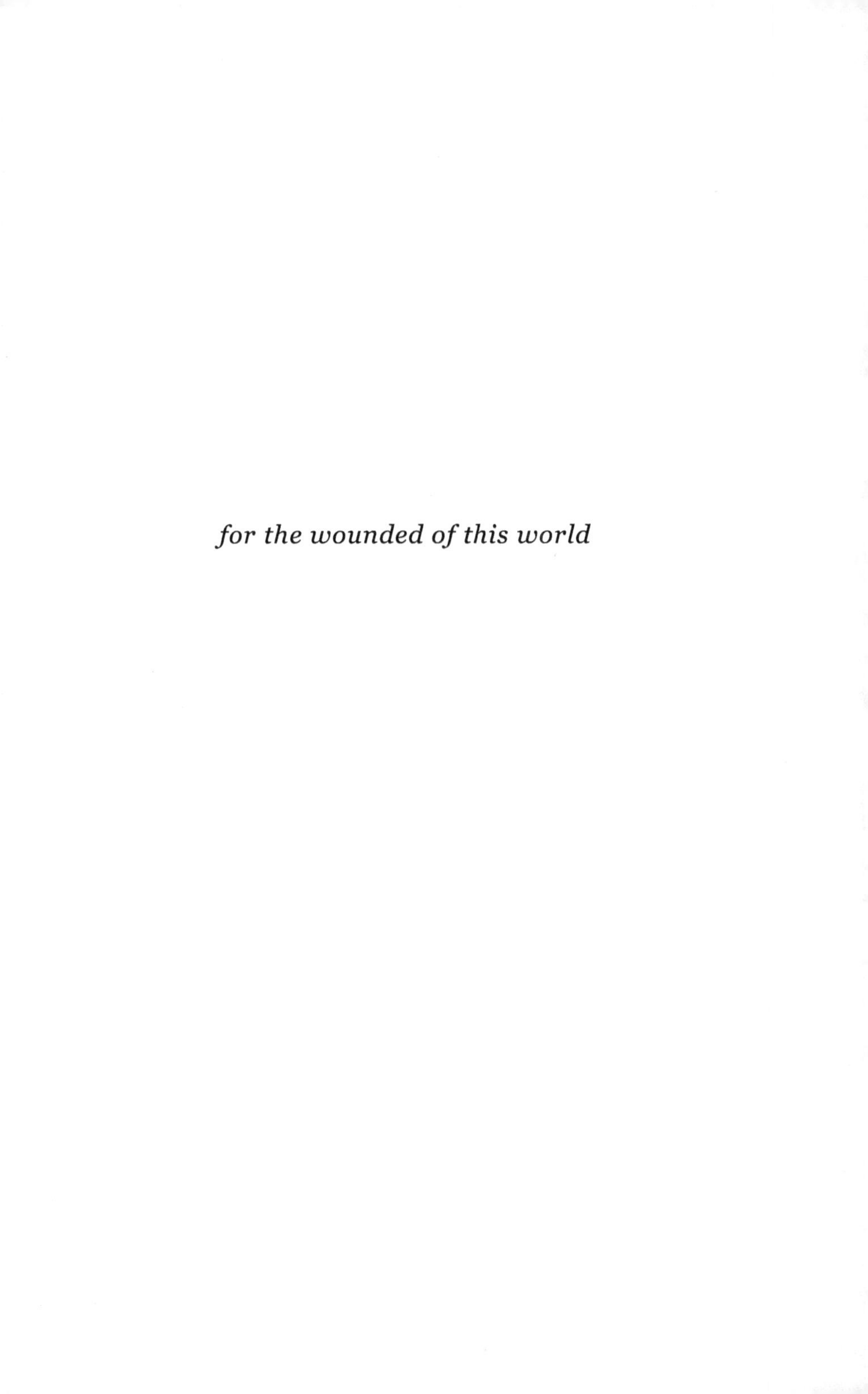

for the wounded of this world

IN ASTROLOGY, THE SKY IS PARCELED into a pie chart of twelve houses. All houses range from 1-30 degrees. In an individual's chart, planets appear somewhere within that range, determined by the moment of the individual's birth.

The weeping degree is an astrological term that refers to the 28-30th degree. When a planet appears at the end of a house, it is said to be in its descent or demise and is described as "weeping." In the final 29th degree—the weeping degree—relationships flounder, plans fall apart, and our dreams escape us.

The following poems and prose are inspired by the weeping degree, significant placements in the author's chart, and the Sabian Symbols. The Sabian Symbols are a set of phrases, metaphors, and images that correspond with each of the 360 degrees of the wheel of the zodiac, from Aries 1 to Pisces 30. They were channelled in 1925 by the gifted clairvoyant Elsie Wheeler and recorded by Dr. Marc Edmund Jones, a noted American astrologer and spiritualist. They were expanded upon and made popular in the 20th century by astrologer Dane Rudhyar in his book, *An Astrological Mandala: The Cycle of Transformations and Its 360 Symbolic Phases*.

We are born at a given moment, in a given place and, like vintage years of wine, we have the qualities of the year and of the season of which we are born. Astrology does not lay claim to anything more.

~Carl Jung

Astrology is a language. If you understand this language, the sky speaks to you.

~Dane Rudhyar

Contents

PART ONE:

*The Home
For
Little Girls*

The Weeping Degree

*You were born with Pluto, the planet of pain and
transformation, in the Weeping Degree,* the astrologer said.
I went to him to consult the constellations, with epaulettes of
hematite and dread, subway trains rumbling through my hair.

Strange lemmings, lure of the tracks. How easy it would be to
slip onto the rails, surrender this karmic flesh, in the hope of
beginning again anywhere else.

Difficult inception. Late blooming chart.

29th degree—final moment when everything falls apart.
Astrological signature for abandonment and neglect.
Persephone's torment. Message never delivered. A child
unborn. Brilliant ideas the world is too stubborn to want.

So many oppositions. Always a no before the yes.

I confess, I came so close. St. Clair train thundering under his
floors, my shoes shivering with knowledge. Until he showed
me...there are secret tunnels, whole underground cities. Above,
signs in stars.

*Your fate is a cruel master, crucible of the warrior, but God
gave you the name of a Gaelic hunting dog, your own sweet
howl. When it's time, darkness will dance you into light. Your
weeping will sprout roses. Your wounds take flight.*

So, don't kill yourself, okay? Life gets better, I promise.

Sun in Taurus

*In Western Astrology, one's sun sign is determined by where
the sun was in the sky at the time of birth, and in which of the
twelve houses. Many astrologers believe that the sun sign is our
personality, our destiny, and who we are learning to be in this life.*

~Michael Zizis, Astrologer

On the day I am born,
five planets
station retrograde.

The earth stands still.
The self turns inward
for a life of reflection.

Sun in Taurus
April 24th
I am 04 degrees.

Mother Nature's own.
Beauty and the Beast.
Conjured offspring

between a prom queen
and a jazz beatnik
on a drunken night

under barn light. To the serenade
of Louis Armstrong, Duke Ellington,
and Charlie Parker.

Sent to seek and sing.
I am a Friday in April—trilliums,
hyacinths, and daffodils.

The crescent moon and how
I will always love
beginnings better

than endings. Comingling of
the constellations: bull, sad sisters,
the fish and the twins,

I am a month of rain and thunderstorms.
I wear pink Keds, black patent Mary Janes,
slap white sneakers through puddles

and if they get dirty
                 I DON'T CARE!
At six, I will climb maples, oaks,

and elms, wrap my arms around bark,
sure that trees can hear
my thoughts.

Drink lemonade and
chocolate milk by
the gallon. Regular milk

out of the carton.
As an adult, I will learn to say *merci,*
dhanyavad, and *gracias,* in that order.

I will travel the world
and stay at home, refuse
to go out.

But before all this,

I am the one-year-old child
in a sepia photograph
smiling on a lawn.

Golden-haired, full of
hope and trust,
before all trust is broken.

I am a lone pink blanket,
beloved first born,
sister too soon of a blue blanket,

a baby boy. I am the neglected one
when the new baby comes.
Forgotten.

The older sister who listens
to the gurgles in the next crib,
wishing the intruder gone.

The jealous child.
Baby cries, then baby
goes quiet, suddenly.

Replaced by a gathering of adults,
black crows sighing condolences.
A forest of legs

nyloned and trousered.
A lady's whisper:
Baby's gone to heaven now...

Afterward, I am the long, empty nights.
The locked door. The hi-fi turned up loud
to cover my mother's sobs.

I am the smell of Rothman's cigarettes,
old kitty litter
and empty Chardonnay bottles.

Still, I am an earth sign,
a fixed sign,
dogged and determined.

I do not give up; learn to rock my crib
when no one comes,
rock and rock

all the way across the room
until it shatters, trapping
my leg in the rails,

blocking the door. I am stuck
until the fireman climbs in the window.
Then I am forever more the story of the child

whose grandfather will go through
Simpson's department store,
shaking every crib to find one   *sturdy enough.*

Aquarius at the Midheaven:
Leaving Home

*The individual may experience a sudden or unexpected
separation from a parent.*

~Michael Zizis, Astrologer

We take #92 South Woodbine bus to Kingston Road
holding hands all the way
to the Home for Little Girls.
A Sunday outing,
to a simple bungalow
in Scarborough,
on a blanched suburban street
with a single spindly maple
staked to the lawn.

Not a dandelion in sight.

I am delivered like a package to
two strange women—
Rainey and Gabby.
The door slams,
I press my two-year-old cheek
against the screen,
smelling dead flies,
spiders,
and creatures that have
lost their wings.

My mother's heels
click-clack away on the pavement.

She is a blur of beehive
and receding pink cardigan, undone by wind.

My disappearing flesh and blood
becoming indistinct,
doll-sized,
a Barbie.

Every Sunday from here on in,
the shock of my own wailing
will send shivers along my skin.
Still, every week, she turns her face away.

I cry as if I already know I will spend the next
seven years wetting the bed at 3 a.m.,
dreaming in grey, afraid of the man
with the turtle head.

Having nightmares of running out onto the lawn
in cold bare feet—

I open my mouth to call for help,
and scream and scream and scream.

But no sound
comes out.
No
one
hears
me.

Mercury in Aries:
The Home for Little Girls I—
The Backyard

(The individual has) a terrier like mentality... often speaks
before thinking...coming refreshingly to the point.

~*Lyn Birkbeck,* Sun, Moon and Planet Signs

We are sent outside after breakfast. Rain or shine. Winter or
summer. We play outside all day long at the Home for Little
Girls. We pee in the grass, allowed to come in only for number
two breaks. Drifting from swing set to sandbox to a chest
brimming with naked G.I. Joe's and limbless dolls and teddy
bears. Old dresses for dress up. We make up our own stories
to pass the hours. *After all, children need fresh air. The great
outdoors.* We shiver together under the eaves, count the drum
rolls during thunderstorms, blow on each other's fingers to keep
warm.

There's a big backyard at the Home for Little Girls. Room to
roam. But we're more interested in the vegetable garden on
the other side of the fence. The place we're not allowed to go.
Mrs. McKenzie's old farmhouse, a vision from times before.
Bird feeders and fence posts. Cricket sanctuary. The last of
the farmhouses on our street in the suburban maze of the new
concrete subdivision.

In August, Mindy and I crawl on our bellies to stalk the fence;
stick our thieving fingers through the metal and pluck fresh
beans. What a wonder! What a taste! Furry skins, the crunch
between our teeth, the wet squirt of living green. It is always
like this—we steal goodness, no one offers us anything for free.
We giggle and feast guilt-free, until Mrs. McKenzie appears.
Storm cloud hair. Faded tulips on her old house dress. Mouth a
perpetual licorice twist grimace. She spies our sneakers, poking

above the long grass, waving like daisies from our bent legs, giving us away. Flies down the stairs with her broom like the Wicked Witch of the West. Loping through rows of tomatoes and eggplant, shooing us away.

I'm going to tell your mother! she shrieks. We stagger back from the fence but stand our ground.

We have no mothers! Good luck! I shout back. Our mothers don't know our days.

From Sunday to Friday, we are orphans. Invisible cast offs, stowaways. The old lady gives up in defeat and complains all the way back to her house. But, for a moment, we know the invincibility of having nothing and no one.

Pluto in the Fourth House: Your Home is Unsafe

The 4th house sits at the base of the individual's chart and symbolizes home and family. When Pluto, God of the Underworld and Lord of Death, is in the 4th house, this suggests a family and homelife where a person doesn't feel safe.

~*Michael Zizis, Astrologer*

Sheryl comes in jacket weather, spring.
Dandelions nod yellow girly heads,
struggling upwards, from parched insufficient ground.
She appears in the backyard one day,
I do not remember when—
telling me she is six
in two months and two days.
But I am already six and thirty days,
so I win.

> She scowls, hates me openly.
> Indignant despite her tattered
> pedal pushers, her dirty red Keds.
> Missing shoelace.
> Trampled heels.
> Unbrushed, wind-scattered hair.

Blonde and blue-eyed,
she could be my twin.
We stand back-to-back
and measure our heights.
She beats me by
the tip of her baby finger.
I know she's cheating,
standing on tiptoe,

but I don't argue—
we may be friends yet.

> Only, her nose is bent,
> her face pummeled and bruised
> from beatings. Hardened
> already. That stubborn chin,
> wild toughness like a smell.
> *She swears like a sailor,*
> Rainey says.

I'm supposed to look after her,
show her around.
And I do...the playroom, the dormitory,
    then outside to the swing set,
        the toy box and sandbox,
            where little Mindy plays house
                with a doll missing its legs.

> Re-enacting a story we all rehearse:
> Mom and Dad come to get her
> and take her home for good.

Sheryl kicks the sand.
That's for pipsqueaks,
not big girls like me.
Show me something
I might actually like, shitface.

> There's a wind through my heart
> whenever Sheryl's around.
> She's bad news. The hour
> scrambles. When did she come?
> Today? Yesterday? Tomorrow even?
> She blinks at me with

that mirror face.
A girl scarily like me, but not.
A girl I might become
if I were unlucky enough,
to never go home again.

There are things about her I can't quite remember.
And later, things about her I can't quite forget.

For many years she
is just the girl
who came to stay,
then disappeared,
like so many foster kids,
but one who had my likeness
and stalked my memory.
A girl I knew for an afternoon or two.
Playing tour guide. A girl I
tried to impress.

On that day, I open up the toy box,
Pandora's chest—whiff of dirty laundry,
grasshoppers and haunted basements.

Show her the costumes:
housedress, barber's cap,
soldier's coat, clown jumpsuit.
The baseball bat and glove,
two dolls without dresses,
a soccer ball and best of all—
two grey plastic swords
for playing Knights of the Round Table.

She seizes the latter
and waves it about,
then promptly smashes me

on the head, chasing me
around the yard. Whacking me
when I pause or stop.
Not just my sword,
but my head and shoulders,
shouting: *I hate you! I hate you!*
I know what you did!

But what had I done?

I never met you before in my life!
Her jaw dropping, incredulous,
she whacks me once more for good measure

Why are you hitting me?

You know,
       you know?!

       But I don't know. Don't remember.
       On and on around the yard we go
       until I trip, fall backwards,
       shouting: *Stop it! Stop it!*

       It's useless. She doesn't listen.
       Finally, I drop my sword,
       run to the kitchen window,
            coward that I am
                shouting *Rainey, Rainey! Help!*
                    The new girl's gone nuts!

                       But Sheryl won't stop.
                       Fuelled by rage, she beats me into
                       a huddled corner
                       under the window,

where I cower
protecting my head
with skinny six-year-old arms

until Rainey runs out, apron over housedress,
pink plastic gloves still dripping wet,
wrenches the sword away from Sheryl,
and marches the bad girl to the playroom
for a little talk.

What's wrong with the new kid?
Mindy and Darlene whisper,
standing in the sandbox.
The question hanging in the air,
unanswered.

I didn't know then
how time is elastic,
how the past lives on,
loops and traps us.
How denial is so clever.
How fear freezes time like water
to protect us from what's
too painful to remember.

Years later, I hear her accusation:
you know, you know...
and shiver.

When I'm 33-years old
Sheryl returns,
in all her trailer trash fury,
in flashes and shards of memory.
Naked in the playroom
—shrieking and flailing.

I see her mouth opening and closing,
but I can't hear anything,
having slipped under the ice
where fear usurps all sound.

     Frozen owl-eyed
       and watching,
     it takes two adults
       to hold her down.
     She lies on a plastic sheet,
       an old shower curtain,
     on the baby changing table, scattered
       diaper pins, baby wipes,
     blankets pink and yellow.
       But it's too small and
     her scrappy legs dangle,
       even as she kicks and punches,
     scabs on both knees
       bloody with Mercurochrome.

I see she doesn't have a hope in hell.
She smells like campfires
   and old cheese. Neglect.
Mothers who smoke and drink O'Keefe Ale,
   fathers who skip town
with the whole paycheque,
   returning drunk, to beat their children.
She doesn't have a chance.

     The camera captures all this:
     the plastic, the tragic girl,
     Sheryl's near nakedness,
     except for her red Keds,
     the tenderness of the
     trampled heels.

The budding breasts,
too new for open air.

    I am sick
    on seeing them,
    start to choke,
    try to run,
    but Rainey holds me still,
    makes me watch
    the doomed girl,
    forcing me to watch.
    So that I might glimpse
    my own lost future.

        The cameraman's
        trousers drop.
        Sheryl stretches out
        a dirty hand
        to me, imploring:
        Help! Help me!

And I sob, for
suddenly I understand:
you know! *you know*!

    I will weep years of tears
    for that mouthy, forgotten girl,
      the one who clobbered me
    with a plastic sword.

    Her face so like mine—
    for I could not
    help either of us.

The Pleiades, or Seven Weeping Sisters

*In Greek mythology, the Pleiades were the seven daughters of
the Titan Atlas. Forced to hold up the sky for eternity he was
therefore unable to protect his daughters. To save the sisters
from being raped by the hunter Orion, Zeus transformed them
into stars.*

~theconversation.com

Creak of the trapdoor as I tumble down the stairs of the root
cellar, egged on by beefy hands. Land with dirt-smeared cheek,
skinned elbow. Smell of dank basement, mouse pee and despair.
Pray to be safe from spiders and monsters, although it's the
adults upstairs I fear the most. The men's raucous laughter,
stench of beer and Player's cigarettes. Predatory two-leggeds
with revenge in their hearts, still fighting the war. They talk to
their deceased relatives in frames on the dining room sideboard.
There are photos of the living too—Rainey in tricorn hat,
Gabby in the Wrens, navy jacket, gold buttons, kick pleats and
vermillion lipstick. *Never at Sea.* Their half-smiles betray them.
They hurt the better memory of themselves over and over.

I whimper in the darkness as the trapdoor slams shut. Pray to
my Sunday School God. Sing to keep from getting hysterical,
the song my Nana taught me: *Jesus loves me, yes, I know...*
eyes trained on that crack of light, willing it to grow. Willing
sunshine, daylight, goodness, anyone? Maybe Jesus to come
save me. Now!

There's a cackle at dusk. Smell of man sweat and broken horses.
You must break them if you want them to do what they're told,
the pretend uncles warn. Clomp of boots, breath highjacked in
my throat. But they haven't come to feed me or let me out—no!
Instead, they toss something in—it lands on my belly with a
thud like a wet baseball, a punch to the gut. *You miss your
friend. Well, here she i*s! I breathe tiny shallow breaths, meant
to protect me from the truth. Meant to keep me from falling off

31

the edge of the known sane world, into the gaping absence of love. Madness is an abyss from which I might never return.

Is it real? Or just a doll's head?

I lie there so still for what seems like forever, not willing to move or find out. While the warmth seeps into my shorts, and my T-shirt becomes a sticky swamp, I imagine blood trickling down my sides, pooling under my back, taste of copper on my tongue, scent of raw flesh in my nose. Everything goes black, *you know, you know…*you can go temporarily deaf and blind from terror alone. Forget who you are. One becomes two. Develop a shadow self all the bad stuff happens to. Click the lock as the mind just shuts down.

Hours later, I summon the courage to lift my hand, find the cornsilk strands, and stroke her hair. Sing her gently into the next world. *Jesus loves all the children …all the children of this world.* Even white trailer park trash with potty mouths and scabby knees like Sheryl.

When they finally let me out, I'm insanely grateful.

North Node in Scorpio:
The Home for Little Girls II—
I Don't Want to be In Pictures

Sabian Symbol, 2 Degrees Scorpio: A Delicate Bottle Of Perfume
Lies Broken, Releasing Its Fragrance.

       ~Dane Rudhyar, An Astrological Mandala

Someone collects me in the night
   the darkness drips, never safe.

     I leave the smell of sleep and
       urine-soaked sheets. Running dreams.

        Lie down in the backseat to
         listen to the roar of wheels,

           green signs fly. Bye.
            White letters to directions

             I cannot read.
              Blink in the dark

               halo around a lamp
             in the shape of a question mark.

          The noises the night makes on the open road
       while the ordinary

     are dreaming. Safe in their beds.
    Other sounds thunder like nightmares.

   Creaking metal door
 a vast, echoing space.

Lights! Camera!
   Watch the teddy bears

        dangle
            from the ceiling

                glassy-eyed
                    and penitent above.

                The fat man
                    with a clown's nose

                            wears no clothes. He tells me
                                my mother said it was okay.

                    A blonde at the back of the room
                    with a dead face
                    nods and pretends.

                I can't hear for the shrieking of some other girl.
            Can't smell for the pee-pee stink.

        I will cry when my photograph
        is taken for years and years after this,

and not know why.
Why are you so sensitive? my mother will ask.

    I am the dust motes
        on the ceiling.

            I am some other girl who was not raped.
                I am the threats: *If you tell, we'll kill your mother.*

On weekends, she smokes in the double bed beside me,
her cigarette swooping,

a worried red songless bird,
crashing through the ink of night.

I reach for her
in the morning first thing,

relieved to find
her flesh intact,

warm
still breathing.

Relieved.
My silence

has kept her alive
another day.

Neptune in Scorpio:
The Home for Little Girls III—
Only the Nightlight Knows

Sabian Symbol, 4 Degrees Scorpio: A Youth Holding A Lighted Candle In A Devotional Ritual Gains A Sense Of The Great "Other World."

~Dane Rudhyar, An Astrological Mandala

We sleep in a dormitory at the Home for Little Girls. In a row of tidy beds under the eaves. My bed is closest to the window, where I can see the sandbox, metal swings, and Mrs. McKenzie's rows of squash and beans—and beyond—the sweep of beckoning fields.

We say our prayers on our knees at the Home for Little Girls. I list the names of everyone I know and count them on my fingers: Mommy and Nana, Grandpa and Daddy, the people I see and the people I don't see. Ever. Like Daddy, with his cigarette pack rolled into his T-shirt sleeve, and his red Corvette with the busted roof from when he rolled it in a ditch. His radio is always on. Loud. He smells of smoke and Hall's mentholated cough drops, even though he's never sick. He said he'd come back for me one Sunday, but he hasn't yet. I list all my pets, living and dead, ending with Tao the Siamese cat who plays *tag—you're it!* Then I list the other girls—Mindy and Darlene— the ones who are here, and the ones who disappear. The ones whose parents got divorced, went to jail, or just stopped loving them altogether.

We sleep with a night light at the Home for Little Girls. When Gabby turns off the overhead light, she leaves the nightlight on, to scare away the boogieman, that trickster who hides under the housecoats on the closet door or lurks among the dust bunnies under the bed. All night long, the nightlight glows, a steady beacon of yellow hope in the shape of a plastic angel with wings. She shines in the dark, guarding our sighs and dreams.

One night, when I can't get to sleep, I tiptoe across the floor and tell the angel my secrets in a whisper no one can hear. The other girls do it too, taking turns, copying me, their white nightgowns drifting like cotton ghosts across the floor, making a shushing sound. Cupping their small hands, they beg the angel's ear. Who knows what they ask for? My wish is always the same, though.

Only the nightlight knows: *I want to go home. I want to go home. Please, let me go home.*

South Node in Taurus:
The Home for Little Girls IV—
Mindy Departs

Sabian Symbol, 1 Degree Taurus: An Electrical Storm.

> *~Dane Rudhyar,* An Astrological Mandala

I was the last to go home.

Mindy leaves when I am seven or is it six?
Abruptly taken away by her mother,
after tea at her mother's penthouse.
Did she say something? Tattle-tale?

> A long beige hall,
> bright lights at the end,
> windows cast shadows.

> In Mindy's pink bedroom, we play
> Barbie meets Ken, Mindy's favourite game.
> I pretend not to be bored;
> bash in Ken's head.

> Until the mothers call us in.

> Whiff of competing perfume,
> beehives—one blonde, one brunette,
> lean in, conspire together. They address
> yours truly:

*Is anything going on during the weekdays
at the boarding home?* (Mindy spends the weekends with
her Mom too.) *Has anyone hurt you? Touched you
where they shouldn't?*

Mindy has been having nightmares
not eating or sleeping properly...

Is there anything you want to tell Mommy?
my mother asks.

     I blink and leave behind   my own skin.
          The floor drops   out from   under me.
           Gravity's a coward   and flees.

     Fear like a   deep freeze
         wires my teeth.   Shut.

     My brain   is full   of squirrels
         on treadmills   the buzzing of
     electric lamps   outlets sneering.
         My smile hurts.

The mothers sit cross-legged, correct,
nyloned queens, with
coral nail polish.

     How can I explain
     about the single lightbulb
     in the gardening shed?

     The chafing from the restraints on my wrists
     and ankles? How the electric jolt has a car engine
     smell. It bends my back, like a pipe cleaner, makes
      me wet myself. The room goes black and the
     darkness fills with shame.

The voice at my ear tells me it's all my fault,
only bad girls have such things
happen to them. *Bad, bad girl!*

He hisses even now with his mock questions:

What is your name?
   How old are you?
      Where do you live?
         What's one plus one?

The electric zap when I say yes
   or two   or four   or no   or what?

It doesn't matter.
   The right answer
      is always wrong.
         He carries on until I say...

I don't know my name.
   I don't know where I live.

      You remember none of this.
         You were never here.

This never happened.
   No one will believe you if you tell, anyway.

The Kite

An arrangement of planets in the shape of a Grand Trine.
Individuals born with this configuration are often considered
destined, they experience intense suffering and opposition, but
also the overcoming of it.

~Michael Zizis, Astrologer

Home on the weekends
at my mother's apartment,
the landlady's daughter,
Pippa and I play
Up and Down
on the elevators,
cause there's nothing else
to do.

       We pretend we're at
       Simpsons department store.
       Ask our customers in the lobby
       What floor, ma'am?
       Playing conductor,
       so we can press
       the buttons ourselves.

Going up! I announce.
Up
   and
Down.
   Up
and
   Down.

       Eventually, we bore of being good.
       When alone, we push all the

buttons for the top floors,
just for the hell of it.

To feel the whoosh of *Up!*
Hear the roar of
cables sending us soaring,
heavenward,
to the tenth floor.

     Pink Keds like lead
     planted into the floor.
     Oh, the thrill of the
     dizzy drag upwards
     of the elevator at 485 Kingston Road.

Bing! Doors slide open.
Thud! shut close.
We press B for basement.

Going
   down!
And plummet south
to the bottom once more.

     Where my mother and I live
     and share a big backyard,
     with oak trees and three
     mongrel cats in various colours.

Up
   and
down
   we go,
my stomach in my
   throat.

Like this we ride
the poor kids'
roller coaster.
The elevator
at Iron Gate Manor
Saturday mornings.

Until we are caught,
by an old biddy
in a navy wool coat,
squeaky, rubber-soled shoes,
gold cross at her throat.

She scolds us: *I'm an old lady and my legs are not strong.*
I've been waiting twenty-two minutes for this elevator while
you ruffians have been playing on it. Don't think I don't know
what you've been up to— I can see every floor lighting up. This
elevator isn't a toy! I don't know where your parents are, but
I'm going to give them a piece of my mind! Mark my words.
There will be hell to pay, I promise! You bad girls.

I've been told I was bad before.
So, I'm proud of it now.
But Pippa's parents are the landlords,
suddenly we are terrified.
What if my mother
doesn't let me come home
on weekends anymore?

Our fun is over.

The elevator is no longer
our wild ride,
secret rebellion.

But restored to a dour
service contraption
for grouchy oldsters
who don't know our desperate joy.

My mother is spitting mad.
I'm reprimanded
and must apologize to
Mrs. Polinski
forthwith in person.

I do, head bent, penitent, eyes memorizing
the scuffs on my running shoes.

I apologize,
and surprise! Surprise!
Mrs. Polinski invites me in
for cookies and a sermon.
Chocolate chips and Jesus!
Her apartment smells old and is
full of doilies and china ballerinas
from another century.

The radio tuned to a holy roller Bible station.
The Lord loves you if you let him in...
I tell her I have my doubts. I've been praying to
him forever to let me come home and live
with my mother, but he doesn't listen to little girls.
He never calls back or returns my letters.

She inquires about my
mother and father,
and I tell her the whole sob story:
about the folk singer and the Corvette.
How he left us for

another woman, the racetrack
and the open road.

> *Kids these days!* She shakes
> her pin-curled head.
> I agree. *Please and thank you*
> *pass the cookies!*

> I pretend to listen
> to her sermons,
> for hot and home-baked, Betty Crocker fresh
> from the oven, Spoon and Bake.

I take to visiting Mrs. Polinski
every Saturday from then on.
I read the Bible,
pray on my knees,
hands folded
becoming a better version
of myself.

> Promise Jesus
> I will renounce playing

Up
    and
Down.

> And between
> Praise Him and Prayer Hour,
> I convince Mrs. Polinski
> my soul is worth saving.

I beg her to babysit me
after school from 3:30 to 6 p.m.
on weekdays, while my mother is working.
So that I can come home and

live with my mother fulltime
like a normal kid.

    Everyone says yes.
    Surprise! Surprise! Life goes down,
    and then up. Again.
    Bad things turn out
    for the better.
    Who doesn't love a happy ending?
    Hallelujah.
    Praise the Lord and pass the cookies.
    You know.
    Amen.

Moon in Cancer:
Leaving the Home for Little Girls

*Sabian Symbol, 4 Degrees Cancer: A Cat Arguing With A
Mouse.*

~Dane Rudhyar, An Astrological Mandala

On my very last day,
I wear my very best dress,
pink and green gauzy flowers
bloom across my chest,
white stockings.
I do not know
how to put on
garters. They confuse me.
Can I pee once
they're on?

I have to enlist Rainey—
moon-faced, auburn halo of hair—
for help. I adored her once.
She kneels at my feet now,
servile, snaps the rubber clips,
irritated and impatient.
Why can't you figure this out for yourself?
Learned helplessness.
Words I didn't know
but do now.

I watch the top of her head,
spy the grey sprouting there, and think:
Soon I will be free of you.
Your sad house. The pathetic row of beds.
The creepy fake uncles. The nightly dread.

No one will ever hurt me again.
My imperfect guardians
go about their chores in silence,
the house hushed,
repentant.

Held breath. Even Tao, the Siamese cat,
won't play anymore. Just sits in the window,
staring out at everything forbidden, another prisoner.
I am struck with the knowledge,
these women needed me.
I examine my hands in my lap,
for evidence of the miraculous.
Obedient to the last,
waiting for my mother
to come and take me—home!

Whiff of Chanel and Rothman's cigarettes.
Hellloooo! Nervous apologies and hugs,
a million thanks. *Let's keep in touch.*

Never.

All the way home in my mother's
battered blue Valiant, I sing along to the radio
at the top of my lungs:
"Do you know the way to San Jose?
I've been away so long..."
 So long.

Sun Quintile Chiron:
God Speaks to Me in Dreams

*The individual is very gifted at understanding subtle energies,
symbolism and other dimensions of reality.*

~Michael Zizis, Astrologer

Long after I have
returned home
I have a dream,
where the voiceless voice of God
speaks to me:

*This is the true beginning
of your life—
forget everything
that happened before.
Today you are reborn.*

I am only seven years old and do as I'm told:
I will not remember
those drizzle grey days
for another two decades.

Where does it come from
that voiceless voice?
How does
it speak, without making a sound?
How does it know my name, know me?
My birthday? My destiny?
My inner thoughts.
The sad songs I sing
on the swings at the

Home for Little Girls.
How does it know
the beginnings
and endings
of all things
and still
not
protect
me?

PART TWO:

The Buddha & The Pink Futon

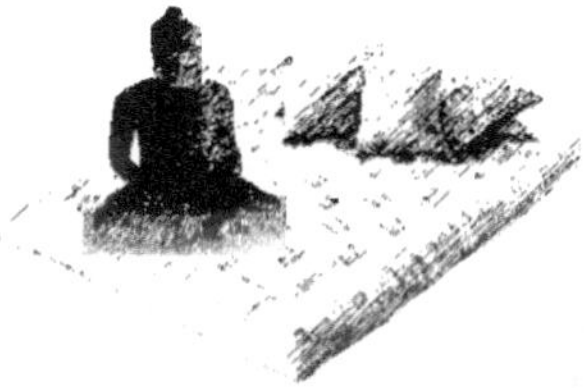

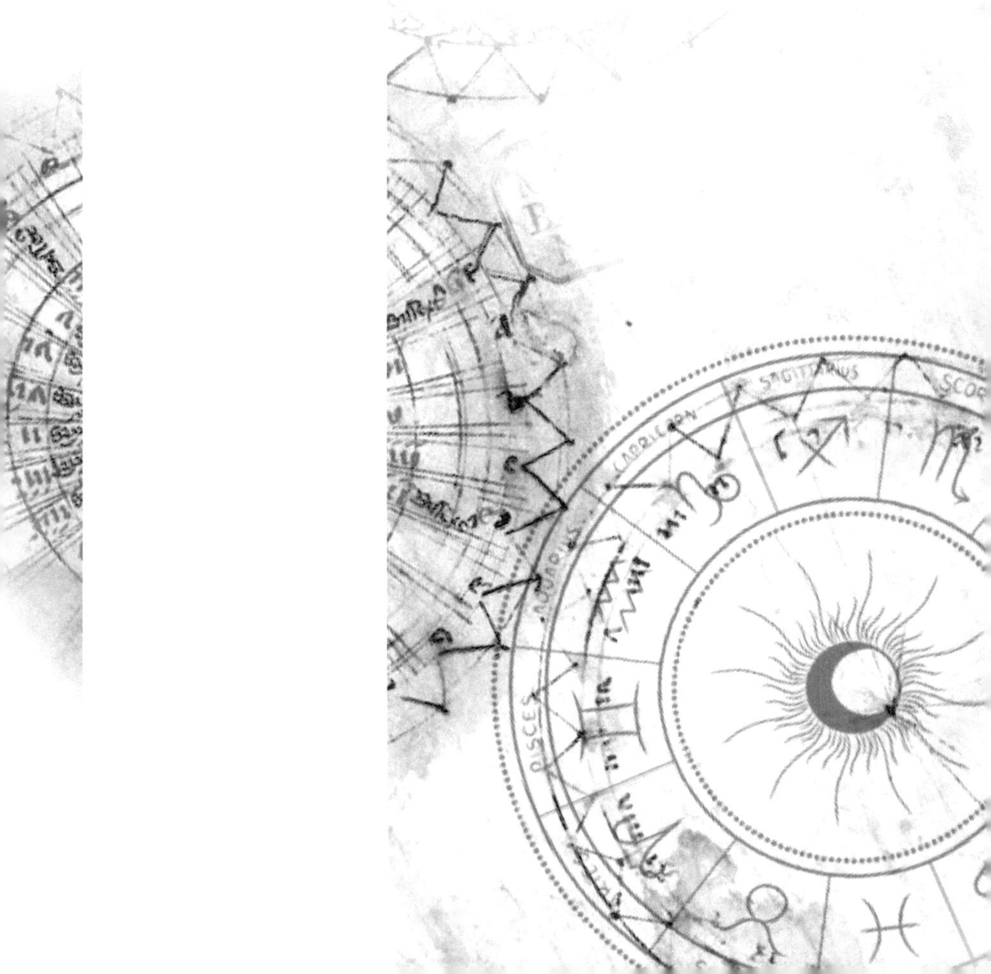

Itchycoo Park

We hang from the maples
stoned on LSD,
in Itchycoo Park at midnight.

Track the moon's smile
as she sails down Rosedale Valley Road,
summoned by the lights of cars.

The faceless drivers blink hello,
they know us. The whole world knows.
The night sky

unveils her manifold secrets
in star bursts, falling stars
with names like: Green Carrot, Microdot,

Purple Heart, and Lucy in the Sky.
Windowpanes and diamonds,
strawberry fields for the fractured soul.

I can hear the earth breathing:
inhale   exhale.
The leaves whisper: *you will be whole.*

My hands leave trails of yellow sunshine,
rainbow smears.
They have always been here,

but I could not see them before now.
Haloes appear, like saints in Medieval paintings
around my friends' faces:

the colour tells me who can be trusted,
and who cannot. The universe is alive
and sends coded messages.

To hear them, I have to climb out
my bedroom window, put boots to bike pedals,
and soar through the night's embracing ink.

Clamber among the rough arms of my deciduous friends,
hang in oaks and elms and maples and laugh
until my cheeks burn.

Dawn arrives with this hilarious truth:

friend/enemy
self/other, past/present
they are the same country.

You were known,
Your essence will always be known—
both happy *and* tormented.

Saturn Opposed Saturn:
I Love You, Farewell

*Transits of Saturn are some of the most karmic transits...This
is an identity crisis that compels you to define the meaning and
importance you assign to life.*

~Corinne Lane, Astrologer

By afternoon,
the girl who looks for
signs in everything takes
the pills one by one. At first,
they are difficult to swallow,
like hard truths, then not hard at all.

Who is this 15-year-old,
who makes wobbly towers
of 222s, then downs
the whole bottle
with gulps of Chardonnay?

   She stole the pale wine from
   her stepfather's office,
   where there's an endlessly
   replenishing supply.
   Popped the cork.
   The good life makes the bad life
   less real. But not for long.

   Fear and sorrow
   are phoenix-like,
   eternally resurrecting,
   feathers flashing, until you greet them
   with open arms.

Blind to possibility, she is frozen inside,
these cold moments of
hot panic. Living in past tense.

She scribbles her final wishes
on an old envelope:
I love you, farewell.
How did she get to this place
of desperation? Despair
follows elation like a tag-along sibling.
Unwanted. She can no longer
manage the doom-filled demons,
who whisper their hot breath
into her ears.

Poems tacked to the wall,
like pinned butterflies. Abandoned scraps
of hope. Messages in a bottle.
Notes of distress, an S.O.S.
in consonants and vowels.

Mars Opposed Pluto: The Funny Farm

The individual seems to find themselves frequently engaged in power struggles of great proportions, and their conflicts are deep and dangerous.

~Michael Zizis, Astrologer

In the hospital they use words like depressive disorder, mental breakdown, suicidal affect, drug addiction—yet don't care that it is too noisy for a person to rest. The whir of the wheels of the rolling trolley, squeak of shoes as a bland-faced nurse strolls the hall, crying, "Medication!" drive her mad. She hands the girl a paper Dixie cup with more pills to save her from the ones she already spent two days puking up. The agony and the ecstasy of having one's stomach *not* pumped.

In the emergency room, all the windows were glazed, one large window made of many opaque squares, and she searched them for answers, but found only more questions. She can't take it back, can't stop apologizing, is always taking up too much space in the world and alternately never taking up enough to be at peace in her own skin. While she vomits codeine-tinged bile into a basin, a nurse tenderly holds her hair. The girl has never felt so sick. Or more grateful. She tells the nameless nurse she loves her, even though she will never see her unnamed helper again.

The next day a friend of her mother's appears to tell her how Jesus saved her from alcoholism. The 15-year-old nods. The earth tilts, life has finally tipped over into the surreal, but she has already prayed to him for years. Jesus is clearly preoccupied with other things. Her mother arrives, sighing, and complains that she doesn't know who her daughter is anymore, or why she's so *hellbent on self-destruction.*

In the ward, the girl seeks solace among the other inmates, repeat offenders, crazy girls all, who laugh too loud and give each other nicknames. Shotput, the pool champion addicted to downers; Sunshine, the beautiful black street girl who smiles when she cries; China Doll, the housewife with the husband whose penis was so big she needed stitches, and who can no longer remember whole decades of her life due to shock treatment. They christen her Wild Child. Give her tips for breaking out of the looney bin. The pay phone is strategically placed opposite the nurse's station. Wild Child begs her parents to promise never to send her for the electric lobotomy. Then cries and tells them she loves them.

The nurses take notes. The girl hopes the doctor will set her free now. She goes to group therapy, takes an IQ test that proves she's slumming it through high school. Learns how to clock, dog the nine, bank and pocket in the pool room. How to hide her pills in her cheek and later spit them into the toilet. Or trade them for Marlboros. How to make pottery ashtrays she will leave behind. All the while, fuming in hot, mute teenage indignation, she learns to trust herself before the medical establishment. Still, she must endure incarceration for thirty days. Who knew it was a crime to hurt yourself?

Saturn Return I

*Saturn Return is an astrological transit that occurs when
the planet Saturn returns to the same place in the sky that it
occupied, at an individual's birth. Saturn, the father of time
and planet of obstacles, is a slow-moving planet, so this major
transit occurs roughly every 29.5 years and signals a period of
growth and life-challenges leading to lasting change.*

~Michael Zizis, Astrologer

Little girls grow breasts and bleed,
but the child remains hidden within,
trapped at the scene of the crime.
Cycles repeat, if
you live long enough.

> Your theme music
> always yours,
> the same notes resound
> in a new order. Like the chiming
> of an Akashic clock:
> *Concerto Adagio Crescendo Diminuendo...*

Outer planets progress
at a turtle's pace.
The divine orchestra
has an orderly progression
with occasional retrogrades,

> synapses, axial loops, your life goes on hold.
> 12 years for Jupiter, the planet of good luck.
> 29 years for Saturn, the planet of challenges.
> 7 years of abundance always followed by
> 7 years of famine and misfortune.

No use railing against calendric Fate.
Degrees of destiny, both squared and conjunct.

Long before you utter a cry,
and long after you gasp and surrender to silent dust,
you will sing among the Spheres,
your sorrow sprout gossamer word-wings.

The Buddha and the Pink Futon

Wings take your Toyota
every Wednesday afternoon
along Dupont Avenue
to the healing room with the Buddhas
and the pink futon.

You have a standing date with
Avalokiteshvara,
Buddha of Compassion,
Lord of Sun and Moon,
who gazes down all-forgiving
with his all-seeing third eye.

His avatar is Suzie,
owl-eyed midwife
of the broken. Mistress
of purification and saintly beings.
She lays her hands
on your heart and tells you
to breathe into hurt.

> *What you resist, persists.*
> *What you accept, surrenders*
> *its gifts.*

> Smell of woodsy incense
> gives you courage. Sandalwood,
> agar wood, frankincense and juniper.
> The body remembers,
> even if you don't want to.

Memory knows no time.
In the quantum universe, there is only NOW.

You cry, scream, rage, say
everything you never got to say.

    It is not your fault, Suzie whispers,
    banishing the blame.

Your once solid self
fissures like ice. There are
shards with their own names,
ages, genders, the keepers
of violation.

You learn to sleep with all the lights on,
Swiss Army knife on the table
beside the bed.
Dream of The Hanged Man.

Awaken to tanks threatening
teenage protesters
in Tiananmen Square.

    Revolution crushed.

What hope is there?
Soak that pink futon a million times
with your salt tears.

    The only way out is through.

No matter. Avalokiteshvara will protect you
from shipwreck, fire, assassins, robbers, and wild beasts.

Pedophiles too? The deity's head once burst with grief at human
wickedness. He cannot be shocked.
His one-thousand arms will pluck you
from any eventuality, neutralize your dangerous karma.

> *To remember is to die and live again.*
> *All tyrants fail.*

Even the one that prattles on
inside your head. The Buddha smiles eternally
as the earth spins.

> *In time, your losses*
> *will become your strengths,*
> Suzie whispers.

And you believe,
that by the grace of the Lord
who sees in all directions,
your extinguishing will become
your hard-won brilliance.

Saturn Return II:
Say Goodbye to Your Old Life

Saturn takes about 28-29 years to come full circle. Therefore, every seven years or so, Saturn will transit, conjunct, square, or oppose a natal point... These periods in our lives can truly feel like lessons. Everything is slowed down—we encounter delays, frustrations, and pressures. But these times also challenge us to face reality, thereby offering us much wisdom and even freedom.

~cafeastrology.com

You don't tell for years. Then, when you start telling you can't stop. Your words take wing like mad confessional grackles. Feathers black and purple, brilliant in the sun. You tell your boyfriend first and he holds your hair while you sob. You tell your mother next, but she says she doesn't know what she did to deserve a kid like you, so you roar away in your red Sunfire—radio blaring righteous tunes, shocked and betrayed. You tell your girlfriends one after the other and none of them knows what to say. Who has heard of people doing such despicable things to children? There is no internet yet. So, you tell your best friend Diane who says *I'm so sorry* and makes you dinner. On Fridays, you watch *Street Legal* together and munch M&M's. Monday mornings, you walk to work through ceaseless traffic, horns assault your ears, escape the steaming concrete into Queen's Park. You need earth, maple leaves. You feel skinless and flayed. You hide in your air-conditioned office all day, the cubby hole with no windows jammed with machines, computer beep, blinking fax machine, ancient photocopier spitting out pages of its own volition. Is it ever quiet? Anywhere? A single desk lamp burns hot light onto the newspaper article you read six times, the words blurring, paragraphs jumping like those Mexican jumping beans you got as a kid. PTSD? You cannot understand anything anymore do words still have meaning when a man rams grownup ____ into child _____? When no one stops when you scream? NO! You are not sure if anything else will ever be relevant again, you are drowning in the past, which refuses to be forgotten, fighting off ghost hands, memory a quicksand, rattling the door of the locked shed. LET. ME. OUT! You cry at the drop of a hat now at everything, misplace your keys and become hysterical in the carwash, you rarely sleep, every day you watch CNN for hours on end, hop channels looking for clues. The Berlin Wall comes down and then you do too. You crack in the bath, crawl onto the black and white Hamilton tile, the whine of rush hour traffic sending you over the edge, praying to Tara the Mother of all Buddhas *HELP! Save me from the noise outside and inside my head.* Next day kind stepfather shows up with a poster of Blue Tara, *just cleaning out closets*, synchronicity? Gasp! Hope glimmers, prayers do get answered, you are living in a liminal world where time dissolves, yesterday bleeds into today, stains tomorrow, your hours a slow burn in your New York style walk-up with the fireplace that doesn't work, beach umbrella in the kitchen, a knife on the bedside table just in case. You quit your job, tell your mother to fuck off, disconnect the phone. So much for telling. Truth. It's Saturn Return. Your old life crashes and burns. You will cry every day for seven years. Write. Pray. Until. Free.

Pluto: Lord of the Underworld

Individuals with Pluto in the 4th house often come from families with complex dynamics. While it is not an absolute rule, this placement is frequently found in the birth charts of those who experienced traumatic or tumultuous conditions during childhood.

~lookupthestars.com

Kidnapped by Pluto,
Lord of the Underworld—
King of Take, rape,
death by poison and decay.

Even when you escape—
you never feel safe.
Such a handsome face,
gold woven through auburn hair,

tall as a stately elm.
Blue arctic eyes.
Long articulate fingers
skilled at stroking and pinching.
Honey voice that whispers: *You belong to me.*

It's true, you will never belong to anyone else.

Not even yourself. *Think of Persephone
trapped in Hades*, the astrologer says.
*How winter comes and the earth withers while
Persephone is held in the demon's lair.*

As a child you
had nightmares of a man
with a turtle's head. Half-man,
half-reptile. Cold-blooded, ancient.

Crotch like skin. Hostile breath.
He chases you in a wheelchair.
Disabled but invincible.

Sticks his fingers where
they shouldn't be,
hissing into your
innocent ear:

Your parents don't want you. You have no family.
You are nobody. You belong to me.

Mercury in Retrograde Aries:
Truth Telling—The Police

Sabian Symbol, 21 Degrees Aries: A Boxer Is Entering The Ring.

~*Dane Rudhyar,* An Astrological Mandala

Years to muster the lion's roar.
Seek justice.

Pick up the phone
squeak

I want to report a crime
plural

to the Ontario Provincial Police.
This after five years

of sleuthing
flipping sepia pages of old

Might's Directories and *Yellow Pages* in stuffy libraries
putting a name to the anonymous voices.

One fat, one thin, two criminal pals
you knew of only as *uncles.*

Another two years
to get the police to see you—

We cannot help you without a name.
It's not like television. *CSI be damned.*

You do the work. Alone.
When you get there, the police

double team. Offer you
stale coffee in Styrofoam.

You blink in the fluorescent glare.
One stares, while the other asks questions.

Hair bristles on your neck,
your stomach twists, as if

you are the suspect.
Only to learn:

The law did not protect you then
someone would have to have witnessed

your rape(s). Or confess for you
to be successful in court.

Child pornography laws
didn't exist in the 1960s.

You are abandoned by history. *Come back,* they say,
when you know more. On the drive home

you pass schoolyards full of children,
eager boy scouts, little girls in pigtails.

Swing sets, teeter-totters,
playgrounds for the predatory.

A game of Home Free for the vicious.
You want to scream: *Watch out!*

Instead, you dial Victim Services,
tell them your historical tale of woe.

Have you been robbed at gunpoint?
Lost your job due to arson or injury?

All this and more!
You want to hurl the phone.

You have lost whole decades,
faith in God and humanity both.

But others cannot see the carnage,
the DNA damage to your soul.

Memory is suspect. But wait, in the newspaper
the story of a baby admitted to hospital

with gonorrhea, who didn't remember
a thing as an adult!

So, on an icy November day
you try once more,

drive alone to the station
sick with flu and a queasy stomach,

praying to not slip into fight or flight or freeze
and manage to do all three on four occasions.

Hysterically sobbing,
clutching snotty Kleenexes.

Grief-stricken
and feverish.

You should have cancelled, but couldn't
bear another wait.

You've already lost
everything through telling.

Your job, your family,
friends.

What greater sacrifice
does the truth demand?

You give the names of
the culprits; the ones you think

you know the best
are already dead.

How did you survive all this?
lady cop asks.

Pepto-Bismol you want to tell her.
Between bouts of suicide and

crying and incense.
You spend your days

studying how to make gold
from life's dread.

Dreaming of—justice,
justice, justice.

Words on the page
lessen the strange.

We need dates, places.
Road signs fly by

illegible in your memory.
You couldn't read yet.

Childhood's endless hours
have no clock, no weekday,

no directions or alphabet.
I'm doing this for the others.

Those nameless victims
are the only real siblings you have.

*We'll investigate and get
back to you,* lady cop says.

Buzz cut. Worried face.
Irish Spring her only perfume.

Her eyes avoid yours.
You may die of this flu, of this day,

of this need to tell and
inability to tell at the same time.

You get in your Sunfire and drive home.
Pass naked trees, the Canadian shield,

snowy highway battered by wind,
evergreens standing

silent
tall

not sharing.
Your stepbrother tells you

there is no such thing
as child pornography.

Ten years later the
internet will prove you right.

Photos of grownups
pop up online like shipwreck flotsam

of people selling children like exotic pets.
Toddler auctions on the internet. In public parks.

By those brown-stained standard issue picnic tables,
Property of the Ministry of the Environment or is it Parks?

For you it is too late.
You will not go far enough,

tarot lady says. *Give up too soon.*
Healing will be your only justice.

Discouragement, despair
are the enemy of the unprotected.

In the hours before dawn, you can still
hear their taunts: *If you tell, no one will believe you.*

Their laughter an opera in hell. Who knew? In a blind world,
their best camouflage was their blatant outrageousness.

The Backlash

Outraged, you dress up
like a raven, a mourner,
an escaped convict.

> Wear black every day
> winter and summer
> combat boots to
> conferences—
> jeans, army jacket, feather earrings—
> uniform for the unspoken war.

Every week there is more
telling, workshops on all the ways
men hurt WOMEN
RISE UP!

> You stomp along Bloor Street
> clutching your notes,
> renewed with purpose.
> Hope is a pen, paper, book.

Meet the battered for coffee
in anonymous cafes.

> Their stories make
> your toes curl.
> But they look as
> ordinary as you.

The tide has turned!
You tell each other.
The truth will out!

Slogans you cling to
like personal life rafts in the
fickle ocean of public opinion.

Until a new phrase appears:
False Memory Syndrome.
Perp invention, you scoff but within months
jobs are lost, conferences close.

The knowing goes underground, silent.

Victims meet in secret basement
rooms, share only nicknames, aliases.
Scratch symbols in the sand,
like the early Christians.
Fear has come back for a last stand.

You want to shout:
false memory syndrome is
false medical science!
There's no such medical condition.

Victims of car accidents
have suffered amnesia from near death
for centuries. But you say it quietly,
and only to your friends.

Privately, you weep to Tara,
to Avalokiteshvara:
How long must we suffer in silence?
How long?

Scorpio in the Fifth House: Death In the Mirror

As a child you felt like the whole world was against you, but it blessed you with a creative mind. You were affected deeply by the death of someone...the native's creative energy is sparked by losing something significant to them.

~caféastrology.com

You will not forget your dead friend,
felled deer, even as her memory
dissipates in the air.
You carry her spirit everywhere.

She lives on in some corner of you
split   in   two. Your breath
will catch when you see the snub nose,
or sneakers with trampled heels in the street.

Could it be? Mortal or immortal you
don't know, but you do know...*you know*...
She will appear to you in dreams
until you remember. She of the potty mouth
and ever-bleeding knees.

You will feel as though you've forgotten
something every time you step outside the door.
Sure there are two of you. A lucky girl
and a doomed girl. The one who goes home to her mother,
and the apartment on Kingston Road; and that other
one doomed to rot in a dirt basement, under a trap door.

People will mistake your name
for hers. Her ghost will always
wear your face. A game of
Knights, a pair of plastic swords.
She still chases you around the yard,
furious and hollering, wearing kitty Band-Aids
and stinking of Mercurochrome.

PART THREE:

Hands Across the World

Saturn in Sagittarius:
Geographical Cure I

Tested in seeking. The serious seeker. Searching for truth. Further education. Purposeful adventures.

~*Lyn Birkbeck,* Sun, Moon and Planet Signs

You seek respite through the geographical cure; run away from home again and again. Renew your passport. Board flights, trains. Someone, somewhere, has an answer. In India, the train belches diesel as it chugs past emerald fields, water buffaloes toiling, women, dark sylphs clad in turquoise saris, balance baskets on their heads as they bend and straighten. You seek a new life in an old world. Your passport will go missing, you will find yourself stranded in Mrs. Bisiwas' Guest House where you meet just the person you need to meet among the chatter of parakeets, and tourists munching cardamom pancakes. A stranger bearing messages: *There's a place I know where you will find peace....*

You answer the call. Find yourself in a massive tent in a monastery in Nepal looking up at a jolly Tibetan Lama who cracks jokes while dispensing Mahayana wisdom in broken English. *Your thoughts are a monkey. You have supermarket mind. You think answer to all your problems is something that comes in a bottle, something you can buy...* The canvas flaps in the lazy wind, bodies shift on their cushions in awkward recognition, while dust motes dance in the stillness. Lulled by the smell of Tibetan incense: sandalwood and frankincense. You drift on a life raft of new words. Cling to the rope. Every moment before has led you here. *You cannot have compassion for others without first having compassion for yourself.* You try to watch your thoughts but behind your closed eyes, there's a terrifying movie reel of red fear and black violence. If anyone knew, you would be locked up. Again.

You might be going crazy. Fear is like a second itchy skin you'd like to shed. This search for the answer will take a lifetime. But isn't it why you came? You resolve to stay sitting on your bean bag cushion, burgundy shawl wrapped around your shoulders to ward off the Himalayan chill. Until there's a ceasefire. Until peace breaks out in sweat on your forehead.

At the gate of the monastery, they haven't quite built yet, there is a mangy dog with two broken hind legs. He greets every new arrival with an assault of barking, bared yellow teeth, dragging his butt through the dirt. Every lunge rips open old sores, creates new ones, perpetuating his misery. Bleeding, even as he insists on guarding his territory. He is ugly. Vicious. Terrifies every new visitor. *Life is suffering*, the Lama says. *Consider the dog...we are our own worst enemy*. You cannot enter the gates of heaven without passing him.

At 6 a.m., you rise to the bell's clang, retake your place in the tent where the monks chant Sanskrit prayers, the soft syllables like lullabies for your anxious breath. Breathe again, inhale, exhale. The day's talk is titled: The Perfect Human Rebirth. Theme: human life is so rare. *As rare as a blind turtle coming up from the deepest ocean for air once every hundred years. Life is for learning lessons.* But you wonder, what was the lesson in all that evil?

Mahayana Retreat Precepts at a Tibetan Buddhist Monastery

1. Refrain from taking life, from killing any living thing. Including insects.

2. Refrain from stealing or taking what is not given.

3. Refrain from the misuse of the senses. (No makeup, jewelry, perfume, or nose rings.)

4. Refrain from eating after mid-day.

5. Refrain from wrongful speech: no lying, gossiping, communicating, including talking, radio, cell phones, or eye contact; from writing or reading letters, or books apart from dharma instructions.

6. Refrain from sexual misconduct or any sexual contact.

7. Refrain from alcohol, drugs or any intoxicants that cloud the mind and dull the wits.

8. Refrain from sitting on high, expensive beds or seats with pride. Avoid sitting on animal skins.

*Adapted from the *General Guidelines for Your Stay* at Kopan Monastery, Nepal.

Sagittarius in the Descendent: Geographical Cure II

In the natural chart, Sagittarius is linked with the ninth house of higher learning. This house is about education, spirituality, long-distance travel, and foreign countries. These life areas serve expansion and help you connect with the universal force beyond the mundane reality.

~advanced.astrology.com

The gong calls you
back to meditation
again and again

    all month long. When
    the 30 days are over,
    you no longer recognize yourself.

        It takes one full moon cycle,
        the monks say, to change the nature
        of your mind. Forever. To become the archer.

        Hour by hour, you learn
        from Lama Yeshe
        to weather the

psychic storm. Sit through
kidnapping, abuse, terror, and torture,
without succumbing to fright, flight or denial.

        You begin to feel, you
        begin to remember.
        You begin. Hour by hour.

While your feet go numb and your face
aches from the dirty string threaded
through the hole of your nose ring.

Shiver in the crisp dawn. Drink chai tea
in silence, while the roosters crow,
and the monkeys howl.

Your bunk neighbour languishing
yellow-eyed with hepatitis,
on the floor beside you.

> In the tent, you don't move for hours except
> to switch ankles, though you travel
> the length of your life.

Laugh and weep.
Stay and surrender
to the cushion.

> While your knees complain
> and your heart breaks, the flies whine
> over and over.

At the end you leave for college, but always
remember this: the Lamas laughing by moonlight.
The Himalayas rising in the morning mist.

> The tender battle
> of thoughts
> inside your skull.

You will take these quiet mornings with you
as you travel the world. Prayer beads on your wrist.
Paint Buddhas on your college dorm wall.

Return each summer like a trained pigeon
to brick monasteries all over the world.
Until the demons of the past,

loosen their claws. Until Pluto moves on
in his slow arc of transformation.
Until you have hope for tomorrow.

Mars in Aquarius:
When Google is Your Only Friend

*Individuals with Mars in Aquarius are some of the loneliest
people. They collect gadgets, embrace altruistic endeavors, and
impersonal digital communities.*

~Michael Zizis, Astrologer

At home, you spend
sleepless nights
perfecting
the art of
rocking the rocking chair
that gets you
nowhere. Still, you cannot
rest.

In a room full of windows
all of them dark, where is the
the doorway?

You gravitate toward the blue screen,
dare to search for others
like yourself.

Is there anyone out there?

Shame is loneliest
before dawn.
You are terrified to even whisper
the words, let alone type them:
rape, sodomy, torture and threats.

You scour the search box
shaking, until you find new allies
under *survivor*. Not the ones
on TV. Real women.
Nurse activists
on a mission to
educate the world.

You email them secret missives:
Help me! Let me help you too!

They have knowledge,
published papers,
diagrams, drawings.
They know the deadly games
predators play.

They have nouns like needles
to pin the perp insect to the page:
-grooming
-trafficking
-entrapment
-brainwashing
-gaslighting
-dissociation
-sex rings
-pornography
-criminal gangs
-ritualized torture

They have banners:
WE ARE TELLING THE WORLD!
WE ARE SPEAKING OUR TRUTH!

Websites dedicated to emancipation.

It's not your fault, they tell you.
Predators know how to turn
children into sex slaves,
twist them into doing things for
which they will forever be ashamed.

They know how to mix just enough
pleasure with the pain.
Know how to make you
blame yourself
so that they are never blamed.

They pick out the hungry ghosts
from the crowd and groom them
with promises and ice cream.

Your hands hover over the keys.
Begin typing letters on the page.

Like this,
one secret at a time,
the world is
changed.

Pluto the Transformer:
Tracking the Perp

*Pluto moves very slowly, maybe only 5 degrees in one lifetime,
but the point of Pluto is evolution; to take us to the far shore
of where we started. If you start off with trauma you progress
to mastery. It's a lifelong evolutionary process from victim to
empowerment.*

~Michael Zizis, Astrologer

In the end you track him down by his voice, that voice you
would know anywhere, wouldn't you? That gravel slouch
insouciant swagger small town Celtic arrogance. Cerulean eyes
that give you hypothermia in minutes. Still, you summon the
lady balls and talk him into meeting, go visit his house wearing
your leopard coat, carrying your tape recorder. Show him
photographs of you as a little girl, glamour pics of your mother
when she looked like Lana Turner. *Maybe you remember us?*
He preferred the little girl. *Bingo!* You are sure it's him but then
doubt yourself. So many calendar years have shivered and gone.
Has he harmed anyone else? Should you call the police? Do you
have enough? Get him to confess?

You confront him on your second meeting at the Coffee Time in
some suburban mall in the city outskirts. Smell of burnt coffee,
cinnamon donuts; sugar spilt across the table. Bells ringing
as the door opens and closes. He wears sunglasses for his rare
eye disease, and you fall for it until you realize, staring into his
mirror shades, that he's wearing them so you can't identify him.
But it was the voice, always the voice. You still hear it in your
head. Mixture of maple syrup and rat poison, seduction, and
threat. Telling you—*You're a nobody, a reject.* He denies all of it.

When you leave you ask the detective to follow him, just in
case. He goes into a convenience store and stands staring at a

row of children's toys: teddy bears and Ookpiks, stuffed dogs and Mattel action figures. You were kind, said it was a family disease. Generational habit. If you were abused, he probably was too. Is he listening to your voice now? Can he hear your words inside his head? Will he live in fear for the rest of his life, worried that you are coming for him, just like you did?

Venus in Pisces: The Gifts of the Wound

*Venus is said to be exalted in Pisces because love and beauty
can find their fullest expression in this sensitive, imaginative,
and compassionate sign. But, as ever, to reach great highs you
may first have to encounter great lows.*

~Lyn Birkbeck, Sun, Moon and Planet Signs

On Thursday afternoons
they come
all the women
like yourself who cannot shed
the ghost hands.

        Whose countries
        have been invaded
        capitols usurped.

        They have lost
        their sovereignty
        over that most sacred of landscapes—
        their own bodies.

We follow self-loathing
like a river, rage
along meridians
until we reach
that great ocean
of collective grief.

        They swim in
        their own indignant
        tears
        cleansed
        and redeemed.

The secret? With enough love,
time and self-forgiveness
everything can be healed.

Private Burial

First the funeral. You make mini caskets out of Glenfiddich boxes. Old tin contraptions once used for holding pencils make excellent doll coffins. Tip out the pens. Paint them black and blue, collage and glue magazine cuttings all over them, Egyptian burial style. Provide everything a dead girl will need in the afterlife: a good dog, a hairbrush, a small pony and sword, cookies galore. Sunsets, graveyards, and purple nail polish. You find an old Barbie at Value Village with platinum hair who looks nothing like Sheryl at six years old, but she will do. You paint her blue eyes black, dab her plastic doll knees with Mercurochrome. Pencil heart on cheek. Give her ripped black tights, punk wardrobe. Silver sprinkles and prayers. You place her carefully in her white tissue-paper bower, close the lid with scotch tape. Tie a knot with pink ribbon. Place the makeshift bower in a little hole in the forest under an old maple. It's not the only one. The forest is littered with these mock burial mounds with buried miniature sarcophagi, for all the things you have lost to violence—friends, family, fortune, future—your sense of self. These effigies are all doll sized. A child's funeral. Teddy bear picnic gone wrong. You bury this one by the light of a full moon. Struck match, sulphur stench. Candle witness. The breeze applauds in the branches. Cover her with earth and pinecones and best wishes. Sing the funeral dirge. Say goodbye and whisper a word of gratitude or two. *May the next life be joyous. May all your enemies burn with regret.* Tears anoint your fingers for the lives of all the other ruined children, the ones less fortunate than yourself. You grieve the life you might have had. Had you never been ...*you know?* You wait until the sadness is covered over with winter snow. Pray for the daffodils to return come spring and run rampant over the ground with their crazy yellow hope.

Pluto in Leo: Ode to Your Lost Life

*Sabian Symbol, 29 Degrees Leo: A Mermaid Emerges From
The Ocean Waves Ready For Rebirth In Human Form.*

~*Dane Rudhyar*, An Astrological Mandala

Hope becomes
the glinting gems
on your gnarly karmic
necklace.

All the hurts
you received and
those you blindly
returned—
even those
that call your name—
do not own the
whole of you.

Know this: even they
will eventually bore you
and skip away. Become
worm food.

Like tumbleweeds of pain
once they've had their say,
they're eclipsed by morning light
chartreuse rays that animate
the truth:
shadows bow before
epiphanies.

Leaving in their dusty wake:
love's
fantastic
catastrophe.

Mars in Aquarius in the Tenth House: The Freedom Fighter

*(The individual) can be a social activist on a small or great,
individual, or collective scale. (They) are motivated by goals
for the common good... It is also highly likely that, at some
stage, (they) will begin to appreciate that certain goals cannot
be attained other than through teamwork.*

~Lyn Birkbeck, Sun, Moon and Planet Signs

You were born with Mars in Aquarius
the water bearer, the freedom fighter.
You need a worthy cause.

Catastrophe breeds agency.

You travel to assemble with others
around the bronze globe
one city block for nations uniting

to fight violence against the girl child.
Me is we. We photograph
ourselves beside the landmark

reflecting yellow/gold/copper
precious metals on a sun-drizzled
day in New York. Taxis honking.

Pedestrians shuffling. Lining up dutifully in rows
to have our purses scanned for weapons,
our faces photographed for entry badges

passports to the halls of light and wisdom
teeming with headscarves, hijabs,
braids, and ponytails.

Armies of the altruistic
six thousand women
whispering in every tongue

the language of liberation.
Gathered here to represent
the unrepresented: child brides, child soldiers,

sex slaves, trafficked girls and boys,
the beaten, raped, silenced, and sold.
Helen Keller was right—

the world is full of suffering
but also full of the overcoming of it.
The disenfranchised have advocates.

Avatars. Angels.
Womyn warriors all.
We fuel up on black coffee and oranges

rush from room to room, sneakers
squeaking, to bear witness to the
atrocities of the blue warrior planet

that befall girls and women.
Listening for solutions.
Turning blue into bronze.

When it's our turn: we
let our voices harmonize.
Someone passes us the

microphone and we open
our mouths wide
and howl.

Survivor Rules

1. You will burst the blood vessels around
   your eyes from crying so hard, then laugh
   hysterically and experience euphoria.

2. Elevate weeping to an art.

3. No one can make the night
   safe again for you but you.
   Set up the barricades. March.

4. Remembering is a form of witnessing.
   You may not get justice in this life,
   but healing is the highest justice of all.

5. Like dreams: if you think
   you can fly, you can.

6. Pray, dream, write, plead
   and sob sincerely for what you need,
   and the universe will answer you in metaphors.

7. Your old life (innocence) will have to die,
   before your new life (experience) can be born.

8. The in between part is called the
   Dark Night of the Sole.
   Wear sensible shoes.

9. Your wounds become your gifts,
   but only if you heal them.

10. Assemble the whole bouquet—
    wounds and gifts; roses and dandelions—
    and you will have your life purpose.

11. Therapy and recovery are umbrellas,
    but nothing stops the rain.

12. It's not what you suffer, but what you tell yourself
    about your suffering that makes the difference.

13. Forgiving yourself is mandatory. Forgiving others is
    optional.

Chiron in Aquarius:
Tragedy Becomes Comedy

*Sabian Symbol, 23 Degrees Aquarius: A Big, Trained Bear
Sitting Down And Waving All Its Paws.*

~Dane Rudhyar, An Astrological Mandala

A director once told me
Comedy is tragedy on fast forward.
He also said:
    Comedy
           is a serious business.

So here is my life on fast forward:
Father leaves brother dies mother has breakdown becomes
alcoholic.
Sent away to boarding unofficial foster Home for Little Girls.
    Pedophiles
        Pedophiles
          Pedophiles
Escape home to live with mom, until mother marries
schizophrenic
pedophile.
With great smile.
Divorce.
Back to foster care, when did I remember to forget?
More pedophiles.
Years pass.
Mother marries doctor. All good. Until the drinking and drugs.
Suicide attempt. Failed.
Boarding school.
Geographical cure x seven years.
Seven more years of terror and crying on futon,
remembering hell.
Escape Hades for rent control apartment near

a busy intersection.
Recover enough to marry at 40. Can't have children. 911.
Career in toilet.
Thirty years in therapy will fix it.
Won't it?

If you don't laugh, you'll cry.

Every week on Suzie's futon,
you end the session by gathering up
all your pedo-enemies.
You put them in a two-toned
1970s Volkswagen van
and throw them off a cliff on the
Ventura highway.
The clatter smash-up and gasoline explosion
are so deeply satisfying—
you do it twice more.
You and Suzie do this
every week for closure, while
Avalokiteshvara looks on.

Before I go I'd just like to
indulge in a little target practice
with their heads.

If you must know, they split like pumpkins.
Seeds everywhere.
You stage multiple incarcerations, torture,
and arrest. They plead and beg.
Who is the scared little girl now?

You write letters to their mothers, wives
and children and burn them. Avail yourself
of all the imaginary bad behaviour

you can stand. No laws are broken.
But fun is had.

Erect imaginary crosses
at junctures of mourning,
on the calendar. Losses marked.

After all, the hexagram for crisis
is also opportunity.
And it knocks.

Sun in Taurus in the Eleventh House:
Felt Protectors

Sabian Symbol, 4 Degrees Taurus: The Pot Of Gold At The End Of The Rainbow.

~Dane Rudhyar, An Astrological Mandala

Felt protectors
for your jagged nerve ends
and chair legs.

But you felt
unprotected when small
all those years ago.

Dead Mums on the step.
Once orange and yellow.
Now winter brown.

There's what you feel now
and what you felt then.

Dried marsh cattails.
Cold angel.
Stone dragon's breath.
Tracks in the snow tell you
something about
what has come and gone.

All the protector deities
you prayed to
protected you from
nothing as a child.

Nor your own inaction
as an adult. Sins of omission and
frozen plans will haunt you. Can you ever
do enough? Scribbles on the page
have their own volition.
Pig alert. Empty sconces.
Think: furniture ends,
puppets, and Valentines.
Blue spruce by
a lonely labyrinth.

You walk out
the broken door.

Round and round with
your question: *Why
such suffering?*
Chicken shit everywhere
is your answer.

Like Hansel and Gretel
you follow the breadcrumbs,
put some in your pockets,
scatter some for the birds, eat others
on your way to the
witches' pot. You will find
your way home, with your five senses.

Dried lavender
no longer relaxes.
But the Tree of Life door mat
still welcomes guests.

Tap, tap, tap,
freed, the chickens

seek you out, come knocking,
with their worn beaks.
Like gossipy old neighbours
they rap on the storm glass door.

They are feathered dinosaurs,
with an avian vocabulary of 35 cries,
different calls for predators
on land and in the sky.

What are they trying to say?

Let me in! Hello!
We know where you are!
We know the secrets of surviving,
wars, calamity, climate change.
Send sunflowers and yoghurt,
small bugs and crusty buns.
We are your friends,
in good times and bad.
Let go of the past,
embrace the generous now.

Chickens will be more
valuable than gold in
the apocalypse to come.
It's the little things that
sustain you.
Through the virus,
the rising body count,
hostilities between nations,
and financial ruin.

You're safe for now,
but for how long?

Once you've known danger,
it never leaves, but continues
lurking, an eternal possibility.

Soft and slippery,
forgiving to the touch.
That thin veil of fabric time,
liminal space between
floor and chair leg.

Protective barrier
between you in the past
and you in the present.
You can only see life
through the rear view
mirror, anyway.

Hello!
Who were you then?
Who are you now?
Who are we together?
Pressed with sticky tape.

Light a stick of champa
long and wood scented.
Sweet burning ritual incense
for the worried and disaffected.

Reflect how time
can slip sideways,
erase the sad days
with sudden gladness.
Reveal to you the safe haven
of the Ever Good inside you,
now and then.

Chiron in the Tenth House:
The Wounded Healer

*The planet Chiron is the sign of the wounded healer. Placed in
the 10th house of career and achievement, conjunct Mars the
planet of action, this signifies an individual whose personal
mission is healing.*

~Michael Zizis, Astrologer

Half man, half horse,
Chiron was rejected
by both parents at birth.

Orphaned beast/child,
adopted by Apollo,
schooled in the healing arts:

medicine, prophecy,
botany, pharmacy,
and astrology.

Trade your immortality
for Prometheus's fire.
The wound is deep

and lasting, but can
be transcended since
the world is a paradox.

Sidereal astrology
versus Tropical?
Two schools of thought.

No one can agree.
In the latter

you are the bull.
In the former
the wounded soldier
in the 29th degree. It's a mystery.
No one knows
for sure.

The weeping degree.
The Underworld. There's no
escaping the tears.

Curse of the Scorpion
as you grow ragged
and stunning,
silver-haired as Saturn.
Golden-eyed as the Sun.
Rotating with the earth,

you age, gathering
Jupiter's extravagant rings,
as you turn.

Walk blindly forward
into tomorrow, scattering
dross turned to gold.
You only become the healer
when you have the wound.

Acknowledgments

FIRST OF ALL, I WANT TO THANK MICHAEL ZIZIS. Besides being a gifted astrologer, Michael is one of my oldest friends. I am grateful for his astrological insights and friendship over these many years. He revealed to me the symmetry in the stars and how our painful experiences can be transmuted through time and effort. I might have given up without his optimism and encouragement.

Secondly, I want to thank Judyth Hill, brilliant poet and teacher. I took several of Judyth's poetry classes during the pandemic. I hadn't written a poem since I was 17, but I had a title and an idea that had been percolating for years, and she encouraged me to keep going. Judyth teaches poetry as a sacred art while also making it accessible and fun. Taking her classes during that dark time transformed a sad time into an inspired time. Much of this book was completed in her unique workshops. As editor extraordinaire of Wild Rising Press, I want to also say thank you for the great notes. Thanks too to writer, editor Cat Parnell of Birch Bark Editing and poet Kim Fahner for help with earlier drafts. And *muchisimas gracias* to Mary Meade, gifted painter and designer, who masterminded the stunning cover. I love it.

"Sun in Taurus" was initially published as "I Am Sun in Taurus" in *Last Stanza Poetry Journal: Issue # 10; Who Are You?* Four other poems, "The Weeping Degree," "Saturn Return: Say Goodbye To Your Old Life," "Private Burial," and "Geographical Cure" were published in *Hamilton Arts and Letters Magazine*, Home and Place, issue 17.2.1, spring 2024.

Special thanks to the poetic *An Astrological Mandala: The Cycle of Transformations and Its 360 Symbolic Phases*,

Raven Dreams Press, (1974) by Dane Rudhyar, astrologer.
I love these mystical, almost holographic messages. Thanks
also to Lyn Birkbeck's terrific books, especially *Sun, Moon
and Planet Signs: An Astrological Guide to Self-Discovery
and Transformation*, Bloomsbury (1990), which was the first
astrology book I ever bought. Many websites were helpful
in researching this book. Thank you to cafeastrology.com,
theconversation.com, lookupthestars.com, advanced.astrology.
com, and astrologer Corinne Lane.

People often don't understand the sophistication of astrology,
having encountered it only in simplified sun sign predictions
in newspapers for years. Having spent time in India, I saw the
role it could play. Ultimately, for me, astrology is about coming
to terms with our fate and finding our purpose in this life. At
a time of despair, it gave me faith in a greater order in the
universe. It has been a wonderful journey, one for which there
is no beginning and no end, like the evolution of the soul itself.

Time for writing this project was made possible by an Ontario
Arts Council recommender grant recommended by—thank you,
thank you—Paul Lisson and Fiona Kinsella, editors of *Hamilton
Arts and Letters Magazine*.

Finally, I want to thank my husband, Allan, who, although
skeptical of signs in the stars, was predicted to come into my life
when he did and has always been supportive of this crazy thing
I love called writing.

Author's Biography

Kelly Watt's most recent book, *The Weeping Degree: How Astrology Saved Me From Suicide,* was published by Wild Rising Press, Colorado, August (2024). The book has won Bronze in poetry with The Wishing Shelf Awards, U.K. (2025); Distinguished Favourite (2nd prize) in the Independent Press Awards, U.S. (2026); and was longlisted for a Hamilton Literary Arts Award in Ontario, Canada (2025). Watt has published two previous books—the gothic novel *Mad Dog,* Doubleday Canada (2001) and the non-fiction mini book, *Camino Meditations*, by Hamilton Stone Editions, U.S. (2014). She has lived in five countries but now divides her time between Ontario and Mexico with her partner and a shy sheepadoodle.

Poet Ezra Pound's quote, "Poetry is news that remains new," aptly befits the poems in *The Weeping Degree*, and the selection of the serif type font, Georgia, for the body text of this powerful poetry collection is an astute match. Indeed, *The New York Times, the Guardian, Telegraph, Wall Street Journal* and the *Independent* are all set in Georgia, for its clarity and sense of immediacy. Designed by Matthew Carter in 1993, inspired by the Scotch Roman designs of the 1800s, Georgia was developed to be immensely readable by dint of the dark, definitive shapes of its characters. Seamlessly blending traditional form with modern notes, this font echoes the author's use of the evocative images and metaphors of astrology to braid ancient understandings through personal story. This font combines beautiful legibility with strength of character and a sense of intimacy: it is as if the poet is sitting by our side, at times whispering, at times, howling her story to us.

The poem's titles are set in Lucida Bright Italic, also a serif font, created as part of the Lucida font family in 1984 by Charles Bigelow and Kris Holmes. Lucida Bright has a brilliant look that comes from high contrast between strong stems and fine hairlines, sharply cut details of serifs and joins, and tight letter fitting. In an interview, designer Bigelow said, "We called our font "Lucida" to suggest it was made out of light. "Lucida" comes from the Latin word lux for light and clarity."

This definitive marriage of sharply etched dark and brilliant light supports the tender, exquisitely wrought balance of trauma and healing in this formidable collection.

www.ingramcontent.com/pod-product-compliance
Lightning Source LLC
Chambersburg PA
CBHW021331060726
47591CB00006B/1971